ideals® FRIENDSHIP

God knew we needed something more
Than budding earth and sky,
And so He sent us friends to love
To lift our hearts and spirits high;

God chose to teach love's wondrous art
Of comfort, cheer that never ends
By giving to the thankful heart
The dear, good gift of faithful friends.

Author Unknown

ISBN 0-8249-1011-7 350

IDEALS—Vol. 39, No. 4 June MCMLXXXII IDEALS (ISSN 0019-137X) is published eight times a year,
February, March, April, June, August, September, November, December
by IDEALS PUBLISHING CORPORATION, 11315 Watertown Plank Road, Milwaukee, Wis. 53226
Second class postage paid at Milwaukee, Wisconsin. Copyright © MCMLXXXII by IDEALS PUBLISHING CORPORATION.
POSTMASTER: Send address changes to Ideals, Post Office Box 2100, Milwaukee, Wis. 53201
All rights reserved. Title IDEALS registered U.S. Patent Office.
Published simultaneously in Canada.

ONE YEAR SUBSCRIPTION—eight consecutive issues as published—$15.95
TWO YEAR SUBSCRIPTION—sixteen consecutive issues as published—$27.95
SINGLE ISSUE—$3.50

Publisher, James A. Kuse
Editor/Ideals, Colleen Callahan Gonring
Associate Editor, Linda Robinson
Production Manager, Mark Brunner
Photographic Editor, Gerald Koser
Copy Editor, Barbara Nevid
Art Editor, Duane Weaver

Petunias

Like little dames both gay and prim,
In soft frilled caps they sit
Along the garden borders trim
Where summer breezes flit,
And all the world is warm and bright
With sun and dew for their delight.

They nod their fair heads to and fro
As o'er some gossip fine.
They serve the bees that come and go
With a sweet sip of wine;
They flutter when the butterflies
Draw near their door in courtly wise

And linger long with graceful ease
And airy complement,
And many humbler guests than these
They greet ere day is spent.
They listen to the pious thrush
And meditate at twilight's hush.

Helen True

A Flower Wedding

Emily Williams Peakes
Circa 1850

I had a glimpse of a wedding
In a dream of a garden old
Where close by a bridal rosebush,
Holly Hock wed Miss Mari Gold.

Madam Pansy was splendid in velvet,
Deepest purple shading to white,
And nearby smiled her young cousin,
Little Miss Ladies' Delight.

The ushers were Bachelor's Buttons.
The maids, the Misses Sweet Pea
And Lilac, were nodding a welcome
To all of the company.

The bride was led in by Poppy;
His coat and small clothes were green.
The service was read quite stiffly
By the Reverend Castor Bean.

China Aster, the caterer, served them
Ambrosia at Four-o'Clock;
Sir Tulip lifted his cup with
"Here's health to Holly Hock."

The bride blushed golden with pleasure
And hope for the future lot.
A blue-eyed maid beside her
Just whispered, "Forget-Me-Not."

Master Bumble Bee buzzed 'gratulations
And wished that their joy might keep;
Then, while Lady's Slipper was dancing,
The flowers nodded off to sleep.

A Smile

A smile can mean fulfillment
Through most any stage of life
Or finding peace with nature
Far away from crowds and strife.

A smile may be approval
Or a hint that one may care;
A smile may be the start of
Two lives that want to share.

A smile can be just passive
Or a pleasantness self-styled;
A smile can show contentment
In both mother and her child.

In taking on life's hurdles,
There's strength for every mile
In the hope of each tomorrow
And another chance to smile.

Irwin William Kaiser

Kay Hoffman

Kay Hoffman first discovered her interest in writing when, as a homemaker and mother of two sons, she taught at a Sunday school and composed short prayer poems and verses for children's programs. Eventually she started the practice of composing a personal verse to accompany her Christmas cards. After she sold her first Christmas poem to Ideals, Mrs. Hoffman's writing avocation was launched. After her husband's death, Mrs. Hoffman remarried but continued to use her former married name as an author. Today, she lives near her birthplace in western Pennsylvania. Now a busy grandmother, she is thankful to have recently witnessed her parents' seventieth wedding anniversary. Most of Mrs. Hoffman's poems are written about everyday experiences. She never ceases to "marvel at the beauty and wonder of God's world" and is "constantly challenged to write words of praise and thanksgiving."

Friendship

Friendship is a handclasp,
Warm and sincere,
A smile that says plainly,
"I'm glad that you're here!"
It's knowing there's someone
Who's always true-blue,
No matter what others
May say about you.

Friendship is sharing
The good and the bad.
It's laughing together
When life's bright and glad.
Sometimes it's sharing
Our hurts and our fears,
Sharing a prayer,
And sharing our tears.

Friendship is giving
Our heart-gifts away.
It's helping another
And wanting no pay.
It's giving a compliment,
Encouragement, too,
Making the sky
A little more blue.
More precious than mountains
Of silver and gold,
Friendship is a gift
That brings blessings untold!

Friends—Old and New

New friends are fine for sunny days,
But this I've found most true:
Old friends are best to have around
When skies are gray or blue,

Old friends with whom we've shared life's joys,
Its laughter, and its tears,
Who know our faults and still have been
True-blue down through the years.

New friends are good to cultivate,
For we should keep in mind
New friends will someday be old friends,
Those extra-special kind!

Place Your Hand in Mine

Place your hand in mind, dear friend,
As on life's way we go.
We'll share life's sunshine and its joys;
We'll bask in friendship's glow

Place your hand in mine, dear friend,
When skies have turned to gray.
We'll share life's sorrow and its tears,
Find strength to meet the day.

Place your hand in mine, dear friend,
In fair or stormy weather.
We'll know the warmth true friendship brings
As we journey on together.

The Little Friendly Things

It's not the fancy costly things
That make the day worthwhile;
It's just the little friendly things
That have the warmest style.

The friendly "hi" of neighbors
Living on your street;
The smile that says "I like you"
On faces that we meet;

A greeting card or letter
From a loved one far or near;
The cup of tea shared with a friend
Brings a time of cheer.

And to a mother's heart
Could there be a gift so grand
As a tiny bunch of dandelions
Clutched in a little hand?

It's not the lavish things of life
That cause the heart to smile;
It's just the little friendly things
That make this life worthwhile!

You Are in My Thoughts

I think about you often
As I go about my day;
Life is not the same, dear friend,
Since you have gone away.

I wonder how you're getting on
In your surroundings new;
I pray that you'll find happiness
In everything you do.

We've shared so many things in life,
You and I together;
Your friendship is a precious gift
In fair or stormy weather.

It goes beyond all saying, friend,
I miss you very much
And hope this little note will help
To keep our hearts in touch.

The Simple Things

I like the simple things of life—
I do not ask for more—
A little house, some useful task,
And flowers round my door.

I do not wish for luxuries,
But this I hold most dear:
A friend who comes to chat awhile
And loved ones ever near,

The softness of the summer sun,
Bright blossoms on a tree,
The sound of children's laughter—
These things bring joy to me.

In youth we ofttimes yearn for things,
Their cost beyond our reach;
But, oh, how wisely do the years
The deeper values teach.

For happiness cannot be found
Along life's tinseled way
But in the many little joys
That surround our lives each day.

I like the simple things of life;
It's here I'm sure to find
That God is walking ever near,
And I have peace of mind!

Bless You, Friend!

Bless you, friend, for being there
Just when I needed you,
For your warm and thoughtful way
So much a part of you.

Bless you, friend, for words of cheer
When skies above were gray;
You gave me hope and made me see
There'd come a brighter day.

And when the clouds had disappeared
And skies again were blue,
You came and shared my happiness,
For you were happy, too.

For all the kindly things you've done
That proved your friendship true,
Bless you, friend; it means so much
To have a friend like you!

A Bowl Full of Summertime

The dictionary defines the strawberry as the fruit of a rosaceous herb of the genus *Fragaria* with an enlarged fleshy receptacle.

What a dull description of one of spring and summer's must sumptuous pleasures! A sweet-to-bursting red, ripe strawberry freshly picked from the plant and placed in the mouth, sun-warmed and luscious. It's almost like tasting the essence of summer—this summer, summers of years gone by, and summers to come. It brings memories of red-lipped children in the berry patch, trying to gather enough berries for Mom's homemade shortcake. Memories such as these undoubtedly caused the saying, "God could have made, but God never did make, a better berry."

Before the colonization of America, Europeans enjoyed dwarf mountain strawberries, the most famous being the French *fraise des bois* or strawberry of the woods. These were usually served with a dash of lemon and a pinch of sugar.

Fresh, plump strawberries became a favorite of the early colonists who ate them plain (dipped in salt or sugar) or in jams, jellies, and tarts. The Indians used the berries for beverages, medicines, and a bread that was probably the ancestor of our strawberry shortcake.

Strawberry festivals long have been an American tradition. It started with the Iroquois Indians who celebrated the end of the long, barren winter with a festival honoring the wild strawberries that grew near Lakes Erie and Ontario. Early American settlers gathered families and friends together in June when the berries were sweet and ripe. A meal might be served, but the main attraction was strawberry shortcake.

Strawberries seem to conjure up as many memories as a family scrapbook: my grandpa proudly bringing baskets, bowls, and buckets from the garden piled high with his huge, home-grown berries; a beach breakfast in Hawaii with strawberries sprinkled with shredded coconut spilling from a freshly scooped-out pineapple shell; a creamy cheesecake crowned with strawberries as the finale of a heart of palm and lobster dinner beneath starry Bahamian skies.

Many claims have been made over the years for the benefits of eating strawberries. They seem to have been favored for curing gout and fevers. It was said that a bath in strawberry water would keep the skin soft and smooth.

The best claim to fame for strawberries is their taste. What else can we eat that tastes so sweet and juicy and yet has only fifty-five to sixty calories per cup? Dedicated munchers can get a lot of nutrition with few calories from these berries.

Why are they called strawberries? There are many theories. One is that the berries seem to be strewn or scattered among the leaves of the plant; in time this "strewberry" became the strawberry. Another popular theory has to do with the Old English word "streaw" which meant hay or straw. The strawberries were usually ripe at the time the hay was mowed. Others believe that they are so named because straw was used as a covering for the berry beds.

It seems almost silly to suggest ways to eat strawberries. They are so perfect in their natural goodness that it may be somewhat downgrading to eat them any other way. But there are many other ways to enjoy them: in strawberry soups, melbas, soufflés, sorbets, ice creams, juleps, jams, jellies, pies, cheesecakes, tarts, parfaits, mousses, shortcake, and more.

Strawberries are also two-faced; they can be most elegant and sophisticated or downright earthy. For elegance, picture this: a fresh pineapple scooped out leaving the shell intact and sliced strawberries mixed with the diced pineapple, dredged with sugar (perhaps sprinkled with Kirsch or champagne) and piled back into the shell. For more down-to-earth eating try washed and hulled berries topped with vanilla yogurt and sprinkled with granola.

Strawberries are good with sour cream and a touch of brown sugar sifted over the top or sweetened with pure maple syrup or topped with chocolate sauce and a scattering of toasted almonds. Try mint strawberries; a little orange juice combined with fresh chopped mint is poured over the berries and confectioners' sugar is sprinkled on top.

For a change try washed and dried, unhulled strawberries with the bottom half dipped in melted chocolate and refrigerated until the chocolate hardens. Float a whole fresh strawberry with the leaf cap left on in a glass of champagne or freeze whole strawberries in ice cubes to serve in frosty summer drinks.

Whatever you do with strawberries, enjoy them to their fullest!

Carol Hammond

June

O queenly month of indolent repose!
I drink thy breath in sips of rare perfume,
As in thy downy lap of clover bloom
I nestle like a drowsy child and doze
The lazy hours away. The zephyr throws
The shifting shuttle of the Summer's loom
And weaves a damask-work of gleam and gloom
Before thy listless feet. The lily blows
A bugle call of fragrance o'er the glade;
And, wheeling into ranks with plume and spear,
Thy harvest armies gather on parade;
While, faint and far away, yet pure and clear,
A voice calls out of alien lands of shade:
All hail the peerless Goddess of the Year!

James Whitcomb Riley

Friendship Garden

She has a name for her garden;
So many plants there were gifts.
She calls her yard Friendship Garden,
And tending it, how her heart lifts!

One gave her boxes of pansies,
Good thoughts, and the promise of cheer;
One brought her potted geraniums
To spread happiness through the year.

One gave her slips, one a rooted
And sweet-scented white violet.
Her garden is filled with the glory
Of friends she can never forget.

So she has a name for the bright spot
Of blossoms where true friendship blends
With memory; in Friendship Garden,
The summer of love never ends!

Anne Campbell

A Garden

A garden is a hallowed spot
Where iris and forget-me-not
Bloom side by side and in between
The ivy's variegated green!

Simple charm surrounds a place
Edged with fragile Queen Anne's lace;
Bright verbena by the fence
Assumes an air of permanence.

Row on row of multihued
Daisies, waiting to be viewed,
Raise their faces to the sky,
Welcoming each passerby.

So designed that even we
May glimpse God's true identity!

Grace E. Easley

A flower is a delicate thing
Yet grows most anywhere;
'Tis just one more example of
God's tender, loving care.

A flower is a hardy thing.
Its root and stem and frond
Hold blossoms high to demonstrate
The strength of friendship's bond.

Ralph Kettner

For Little Girls

The earth grows special flowers for little girls;
Is prodigal with dandelion gold
So a little girl may gather all she wants
And not give anybody cause to scold;
Is lavish with its daisies and its clovers
For making chains, and tucks an unexpected
White rabbit's head into each larkspur blossom
To be discovered when they are selected
For making into bracelets. But flowers
Belong to small girls more than any other,
And the earth is glad when a soft-eyed little girl
And a soft-eyed blossom smile at one another.

Jane Merchant

Come little children everywhere,
  Let's friendly be together.
We have the same sky overhead
  In dark or sunny weather.
We have the same familiar stars
  That shine all night above us.
We have the same dear parent pride
  To shield, protect, and love us.

Plea of the Children

Belle S. Mooney

Come little children everywhere
  From lands that gave us birth,
Let's make our big and beautiful world
  Our paradise on earth.
Let's put away the differences
  That lead to foolish wars;
Let's live together peacefully
  As do our kindly stars.

For all the world's a brotherhood
  If we but make it so,
And flowers of peace in every land
  We plant and let them grow.
So come little children everywhere,
  Let's learn to be good friends
And let us weave in harmony
  Our world's sad tangled ends.

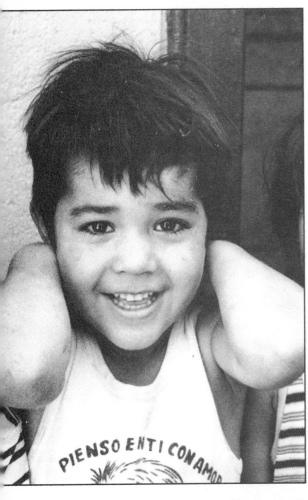

Oh, let us gather for our own
  The best of every land
And mold it into benisons
  All tongues may understand.
When childhood days are over, then
  O'er land and sea shall shine
Most cherished boon of all mankind—
  World peace for yours and mine.

To Be a Child

Garnett Ann Schultz

To be a child is a magic real;
It's different from anything grownups feel,
Knowing, believing, and dreaming dreams;
It's hills to climb and flowing streams.

To be a child is a privilege rare;
There's nothing else that can quite compare.
It's miracles, magic, and let's pretend,
Golden moments that never end.

There are elves and fairies and beauties rare,
A courage real that just children share,
A secret place where you love to go
Where the day is bright and the wild flowers grow.

Nothing impossible, joys so complete,
A peace and contentment and moments sweet,
Eyes ever smiling, dreams running wild,
It's life's sweetest blessing—to be a child.

Summer Vacation

The youngsters are so happy
For vacation time is here,
And every day's a holiday
Filled with joy and cheer.

Their merry laughter echoes
From early morn till night
As special dreams come true
To every heart's delight.

Each path the children follow
Has magic all its own,
And glowing seeds of pleasure
Are daily shared and sown.

While summer's golden melody
Casts its spell so sweet,
Happy children all agree
Vacation's quite a treat.

LaVerne P. Larson

The Dog

As Seen by the Cat

Oliver Herford

The dog is black or white or brown
And sometimes spotted like a clown.
He loves to make a foolish noise
And human company enjoys.

The human people pat his head
And teach him to pretend he's dead
And beg and fetch and carry, too—
Things that no well-bred cat will do.

At human jokes, however stale,
He jumps about and wags his tail,
And human people clap their hands
And think he really understands.

They say "good dog" to him. To us
They say "poor puss" and make no fuss.
Why dogs are "good" and cats are "poor"
I fail to understand, I'm sure.

To someone very good and just
Who has proved worthy of her trust,
A cat will sometimes condescend;
The dog is everybody's friend!

Tenting Tonight, Anyone?

F. Wallace Patch

I suspect I may have spent more nights sleeping out in a tent than many forest rangers or safari guides. I make that claim even though more than fifty years have passed since the last time I did so. That extended experience I will never forget, and, because of it, the last thing I do before drifting into dreamland each night is to thank God for my comfortable bed, the four walls which surround it, and a firm roof overhead.

My introduction to night life under the stars began when I was only nine years old. My father, a dedicated young physician, was motivated by high regard for the widely accepted rewards of Spartan living; and my younger brother and I were often pressed into service as guinea pigs for his health experiments. Although we had found it hard to go along with Father's contention that sleeping on the floor (as he himself did) could make us supermen, we accepted an alternate proposal which involved sleeping out in a tent every night, summer and winter.

Despite the fact that Father's plan for sleeping in a tent was suggested more than a generation before the lure of camping out was popularized, we agreed to do it. It savored of daring, plus the promise of freedom from discipline in such matters as talking to each other as long as we could stay awake, guessing what caused strange sounds, or just looking out at the moon.

Our tent was set up about sixty feet from our house at the edge of a small back lawn, bordering an extensive forest area. Quite often during winter, we had to run through snow to and from the tent, sometimes in sub-zero weather. There were mornings when we had to shovel a path before we could get in for breakfast. To be perfectly honest, however, we never suffered from the cold because, about an hour before curfew, we put stone-crock "pigs" filled with hot water into our beds. With such long-lasting supplementary heat, we were kept warm until morning and never suffered bad colds.

Strange as it may seem, summer months were the ones which burdened us most with problems and anxieties. Ants and spiders were only minor irritants, but mosquitoes were a constant annoyance. All night they droned their whining symphony as they cruised back and forth outside our protective netting. Every so often one would break through the barrier, sending us into breakfast with a swollen lip or half-closed eye.

After midsummer we were constantly serenaded by crickets, katydids, and tree toads; I doubt if anyone who has not experienced it firsthand can imagine how loud and persistent is the constant chatter from these creatures of the night. While crickets chirped at ground level, often right under our beds, the others kept up their raucous seesaw songs in tree branches which reached out over the tent. Loud though this chorus surely was, its humdrum monotony would somehow lull us to sleep.

Another soporific sound, startling at first if it came on suddenly, was the drumbeat of heavy rain on the tent fly. Continued for long, however, this would put us back to sleep, sometimes to dream of passing freight trains. Thunder and lightning were something else! If such storms were not too close or too loud, we'd usually endure them by merely pulling blankets over our heads, but when flashes began lighting up the tent at close range, we weren't ashamed to make a mad dash for the more substantial security of the house.

In autumn we were sometimes awakened and frightened by the multiple barking of dog packs racing through the woods in pursuit of wild game. We scarcely breathed as this tumult drew nearer, then sighed with relief and went back to sleep after fading sound indicated a change of the hunt's direction away from our fragile sanctuary. I also recall vividly the strange call of laughing owls which stirred feelings of loneliness, certainly no laughing matter.

The one period of our year-long sleepouts which invokes mostly pleasant memories, which I would not mind reliving, came during the early weeks of spring. It was then we could listen to the music of water running over stones in a woodland brook filled with melted snow from the higher hills beyond. We breathed a new kind of air which almost tasted of clean, frost-free earth and the first green growth, signifying the turn from hibernation to active life. Very early each morning, we ourselves were reawakened by the cheerful singing of robins. All this we could enjoy long before the mosquitoes returned to pester us.

A healthier way of life? I'm still not convinced that sleeping in a tent throughout the year, without an occasional shift into conventional quarters, offers more benefits than drawbacks. If it is done in spring or early summer, however, chances are it will be refreshing and rewarding.

Friendship Bouquet

Clement C. Moore

These new-culled blossoms which I send,
With breath so sweet and tints so gay,
I truly know not, my kind friend,
In Flora's language what they say;

Nor which one hue I should select,
Nor how they all should be combined,
That at a glance you might detect
The true emotions of my mind.

But, as the rainbow's varied hues
If mingled in proportions right
All their distinctive radiance lose
And only show unspotted white;

Thus, into one, I would combine
These colors that so various gleam,
And bid this offering only shine
With friendship's pure and tranquil beam.

There is a flower within my heart,
Daisy, Daisy!
Planted one day by a glancing dart,
Planted by Daisy Bell.
Whether she loves me or loves me not,
Sometimes it's hard to tell;
Yet I am longing to share the lot
Of beautiful Daisy Bell!

Daisy, Daisy, give me your answer, do!
I'm half crazy, all for the love of you.
It won't be a stylish marriage;
I can't afford a carriage,
But you'll look sweet upon the seat
Of a bicycle built for two!

Daisy Bell

Harry Dacre

We will go tandem as man and wife,
Daisy, Daisy!
Peddling away down the road of life,
I and my Daisy Bell!
When the road's dark, we can both despise
Policemen and lamps as well;
There are bright lights in the dazzling eyes
Of beautiful Daisy Bell!

I will stand by you in "wheel" or woe,
Daisy, Daisy!
You'll be the belle which I'll ring, you know,
Sweet little Daisy Bell!
You'll take the lead in each trip we take;
Then, if I don't do well,
I will permit you to use the brake,
My beautiful Daisy Bell!

Welcome Signs

Her home abounds in welcome signs
That help my neighbor say,
"Come, share a cup of tea with me
To brighten up the day."

She waves a welcome from her porch.
Fresh bread helps scent the air;
Her house is warm and cozylike,
And I find friendship there.

Oak rockers lend a comfort-touch,
And books are all about;
A fern upon a four-foot stand
Spreads leafy branches out.

She never seems so pressed for time
As many people are.
She emanates a natural grace
That says, "Come as you are."

Her welcome signs are true concern
And cookie jars filled high
And interest in her fellowman
That grows as years pass by.

Craig E. Sathoff

The Meaning of a Letter

Messenger of Sympathy and Love
Servant of Parted Friends
Consoler of the Lonely
Bond of the Scattered Family
Enlarger of the Common Life
Carrier of News and Knowledge
Instrument of Trade and Industry
Promoter of Mutual Acquaintance
of Peace and Good Will

Inscribed on the United States
Post Office in Washington, D.C.

The Postscript

Her letter told him just the usual things
Of health and weather; there was little news.
It rained last night, and birds were splashing wings
This morning by the walk where larkspur blues
Leaned over little pools; she was afraid
Of thunder when he was not there with her.
She wrote, "The village gossip called and stayed
Until she learned just why and where you were,"

And then, with love, her name—and close below
The postscript as if suddenly her heart
Had spoken out! A little slanting row
Of words with which he lingered there apart
As once, through slanted cedars on a height,
He looked and found a world all warm and bright.

Glenn Ward Dresbach

Grandma

Elinor DeWire

Grandma's the smell of a jar full of cookies;
She's a downy-soft pillow for my head;
She's a cozy warm kitchen on a winter's night
When I'm yawning and ready for bed.

She's a fairy tale in the big rocking chair,
From a book whose edges are worn;
Somehow I know the pages and words
Have been read many times before.

My grandma's the keys of an old piano;
She's the ticking of the mantel clock;
She's geraniums on the windowsill
Or a doll made from a worn-out sock.

Grandma is a song always humming
Or a clothes basket full of the cat;
Grandma's a drawer in the corner cupboard,
Full of pencils, crayons, and this and that.

She's a candy jar full of peppermint sticks
Or a handkerchief edged with lace;
She's the dusty old attic where I like to play;
She's the jewels in a gold inlaid case.

Grandma's a basket of meadow-grown daisies;
She's grassy old shoes on the back steps;
Grandma's a bowl of rosy ripe apples
Or old pictures and letters she's kept.

Grandma's a screen door slamming shut;
She's a sampler framed on the wall;
Grandma's the teakettle whistling a song;
She's an old-fashioned porcelain doll.

Grandma's the snapping of garden green beans;
She's a begonia in a cracked flowerpot;
Grandma is the glow of a hurricane lamp
Or an apron with yellow polka dots.

Grandma's a big heavy quilt on cold nights;
She's the smell of yeast and rising dough;
She's potato pancakes or marshmallow fudge
Or a porch swing idling to and fro.

Grandma's the sizzle of bacon strips
And the wind whipping fresh, clean sheets;
She's a tiny glass ballerina on a music box
And the smell of a Sunday roast beef.

Grandma is the music of our childhood,
A gentle reminder, while we're young,
Of things we love and things we keep
And things that are to come.

Friendship Tapestry

Special Thoughts About Friends

There is a destiny that makes us brothers;
None goes his way alone.
All that we send into the lives of others
Comes back into our own.
I care not what his temples or his creeds,
One thing holds firm and fast,
That into his fateful heap of days and deeds
The soul of man is cast.

Edwin Markham

Friendship resembles trees
Which are always green
And which bear
Fruit and blossoms
At the same time.

Bernardin De Saint-Pierre

A friend is a present
You give yourself.

Robert Louis Stevenson

It is pleasant
To have people love you
Even when they don't know you,
But of more value
Is the love of the friend
Who has found you out
And still loves you.

Author Unknown

A gentle man is one
Who thinks more
Of other people's feelings
Than of his own rights,
And more of other people's rights
Than his own feelings.

Chesterfield

Happy is the house
That shelters a friend.

Ralph Waldo Emerson

Friendship is an open door,
Compassion, kindness, grace, and more.
Friends, though few and far apart,
Bring thoughts and kindness to the heart.

A. Scott-Donnelly

Under the magnetism
Of friendship,
The modest man becomes bold; the shy, confident;
The lazy, active;
Or the impetuous, prudent and peaceful.

William Makepeace Thackeray

Choose your friends
From among those who
Are faithful to themselves,
For they will also be
Faithful toward others.

Author Unknown

Oh,. loving words are not hard to say
If the heart be loving too,
And the kinder the thoughts you give to others,
The kinder their thoughts of you.

Author Unknown

My life is
A chronicle of friendship.
My friends,
All those about me,
Create my world anew each day.
Without their loving care,
All the courage I could summon
Would not suffice to keep
My heart strong for life.
But, like Stevenson,
I know it is better
To do things
Than to imagine them.

Helen Keller

The most valuable antiques are old friends.

E. B. Birkenbeuel

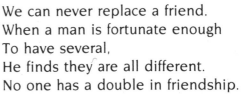

There is in friendship
Something of all relations
And something above them all.
It is the golden thread
That ties the heart
Of the world.

John Evelyn

We can never replace a friend.
When a man is fortunate enough
To have several,
He finds they are all different.
No one has a double in friendship.

Schiller

You'll never offend a person
By returning a smile.

Author Unknown

It's a heap of satisfaction
When a helping hand you lend
Just to know someone's happier
'Cause you paused to be a friend.

Author Unknown

Greater love hath
No man than this,
That a man lay down his life
For his friends.

John 15:13

Oh, to have a birthday!
Candles burning bright,
Eyes so blue and sparkling,
Happy heart so light!

Lois Lenski

A Birthday Is ...

A birthday is very special
　No matter what the age.
It's a day for celebration
　As you turn another page.

Three hundred days plus sixty-five,
　All rolled into a year,
Each and every one, a birthday
　That someone will revere!

There's a cake with glowing candles
　And lots of ice cream, too,
With friends all gathered round to sing
　"Happy birthday to you."

What a happy celebration!
　What joy a birthday brings!
Its twenty-four exciting hours
　Are filled with many things.

There are gaily wrapped packages
　And lovely greeting cards,
Funny ones or sentimental,
　All sent with best regards.

A birthday is the lovely day
　We think of as our own;
May this one be the happiest
　That you have ever known!

Donita M. Dyer

The Waving Girl

Wanda M. Trawick

The young seaman watched the fading lights of Savannah as the freighter made its way slowly through the river toward the Atlantic. Although excited about his first trip aboard an oceangoing ship, he was already feeling homesick as he pulled up the collar of his jacket against the stiff breeze and peered into the blackness ahead. He shivered and moved away from the rail. His duties on deck were done, and he began making his way down to his quarters.

A husky boatswain met him at the bottom of the ladder. "Hold it, lad. Where do you think you're going?"

The boy bit his lip nervously. "I'm off duty now, sir. I was just going to turn in."

The man's eyes searched the boy's face and took note of his drooping shoulders. "Now that would be awfully rude of a young fellow, wouldn't it?" he asked. He clamped a calloused hand on the youngster's shoulder and turned him around. "There's a young lady to see you off," he said. "You don't want to miss her farewell, do you?"

Startled and afraid to argue, the young man stumbled back up the ladder. The boatswain must be playing a joke of some kind on him. Being from the hill country of north Georgia, the boy knew no one in Savannah. Besides they were away from the city now, and it was pitch black outside.

The older man marched him along the deck to the starboard side of the ship. The light from the Elba lighthouse shone ahead of them. The man stopped, leaned against the railing, and nodded toward the lighthouse. "She'll be waiting up there to give you a send-off."

The boy stared at him. "Who?" he croaked. "Who is going to be out there in the middle of the night? And how could I see her, even if she was?"

"You won't be able to see her," replied the boatswain, "but you'll see her lantern. She'll be standing on the porch of the lightkeeper's cottage swinging her lamp. Just keep watching."

Still expecting some joke, the seaman stared at the darker land mass on the horizon below the beacon light. Was that a flicker of light near the shoreline? Or was it his imagination? No. It was a lantern swinging in the darkness!

The boy jumped in startled surprise at a sudden blast of the ship's whistle. "What was that for?" he asked.

The boatswain nodded toward the bobbing light. "We're answering her greeting," he replied. "Who is she?"

The older sailor pulled his collar up against the chill and hunched over the railing. "I've heard her name, but I don't recall it. We just call her the waving girl. They say her fiance was a sailor, and when his ship left Savannah, she promised him she would greet every ship that entered and left the port until he got home."

He stuffed his hands in his pockets and glanced at the boy. "Kind of sad, though. She's been keeping her promise for years and years, but he's never come back."

They watched in silence as the light slowly disappeared. The boy tried to sort out his feelings. It had felt good to see the waving light and know that someone cared enough to bid them farewell in the middle of a dark, cold night, but the story behind her actions saddened him. "Do you think it's true about her fiance?" he asked.

The man grinned. "I don't know, lad. That's the story everyone tells about her. Maybe it's true, or maybe it's just a legend. Every sailor that leaves this port counts on seeing her wave a big white cloth in the daytime or her lantern at night. I never heard of her missing a single passing ship."

They bid one another good-night, and the boy started briskly down the ladder. His shoulders no longer drooped, and he whistled a gentle tune.

On the shore, Florence Martus dimmed her lantern and set it by the door of the cottage where she lived with her brother who kept the lights on the Savannah River. She wondered briefly about the men on the ship which had just passed. Were they lonely? Perhaps her greeting had lifted some sailors' spirits.

She slipped out of her warm robe and slippers and slid between the covers of her bed. A smile crossed her face as she thought of the romantic legend the sailors and the people of Savannah were telling about her. She had tried once to explain her faithfulness in greeting and bidding farewell to the ships.

"It's lonely on the island for a girl, so I started to wave at ships which passed. They began to return the greeting, and now they watch for me."

She was just one lonely girl reaching out to others in the only way she could. For forty-four years Florence Martus, the waving girl, kept her vigil. When her brother retired as lightkeeper in 1931, she was a celebrity among seamen from around the world—a simple girl overcoming her own loneliness by reaching out to cheer others.

"A man that hath friends must show himself friendly."

HER IMMORTALITY STEMS FROM HER FRIENDLY GREETING TO PASSING SHIPS, A WELCOME TO STRANGERS ENTERING THE PORT AND A FAREWELL TO WAVE THEM SAFELY ONWARD

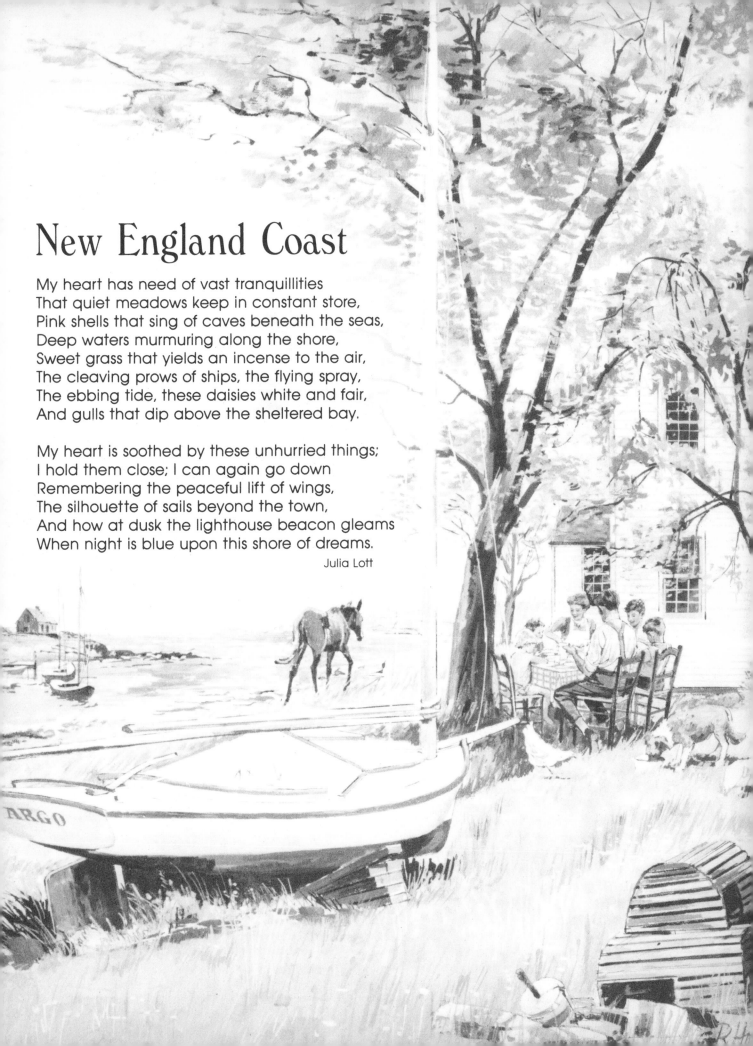

New England Coast

My heart has need of vast tranquillities
That quiet meadows keep in constant store,
Pink shells that sing of caves beneath the seas,
Deep waters murmuring along the shore,
Sweet grass that yields an incense to the air,
The cleaving prows of ships, the flying spray,
The ebbing tide, these daisies white and fair,
And gulls that dip above the sheltered bay.

My heart is soothed by these unhurried things;
I hold them close; I can again go down
Remembering the peaceful lift of wings,
The silhouette of sails beyond the town,
And how at dusk the lighthouse beacon gleams
When night is blue upon this shore of dreams.

Julia Lott

There's a time each year that we always hold dear,
Good old summertime,
With the birds and the trees and the sweet-scented breezes,
Good old summertime;
When your day's work is over, then you are in clover,
And life is one beautiful rhyme.
No trouble annoying, each one is enjoying
The good old summertime.

In the Good Old Summertime

In the good old summertime,
In the good old summertime,
Strolling through the shady lanes
With your baby mine,
You hold her hand; she holds yours,
And that's a very good sign
That she's your tootsey-wootsey
In the good old summertime.

To swim in the pool, you'd play hooky from school,
Good old summertime;
You'd play ring-a-rosy with Jim, Kate and Josie,
Good old summertime.
Those days full of pleasure we now fondly treasure,
When we never thought it a crime
To go stealing cherries with faces brown as berries,
Good old summertime.

Ren Shields

Love Flourishes

As long as love flourishes in the center of your heart, you are young. So long as you radiate beauty, hope, cheer, courage to your fellowmen, so long you are young.

The continuity of life is never broken; the river flows onward and is lost to our sight; but under its new horizon it carries the same waters which it gathered under ours, and its unseen valleys are made glad by the offerings which are borne down to them from the past—flowers, perchance, the germs of which its own waves had planted on the banks of Time.

John Greenleaf Whittier

Trees

Oldest of friends, the trees!
Ere fire came, or iron,
Or the shimmering corn;
When the earth mist was dank,
Ere the promise of dawn,
From the slime, from the muck—
Trees!

Nearest of friends, the trees!
They shield us from storm
And brighten our hearths;
They bring to our tables
The autumn's fine gold;
They carol our joys
And sing to our griefs.
They cradle our young
And coffin our dead,
Nearest of friends,
The trees!

Truest of friends, the trees!
Men wander far
At a word or a nod.
Life is a grief;
Love is a chance;
Faith stumbles oft;
Joy is soon past—
Oldest of friends,
Nearest of friends,
Truest of friends,
The trees!

Thomas Curtis Clark

Oak Trees

Oak trees, how stately do they grow,
Like old dowagers in a row.
They have a pride too, I declare;
You'd almost think they were aware
Of their importance, if you please,
Their prestige in the world of trees.

Whene'er I see a spreading oak,
I think of common sturdy folk,
Of an old room with a beamed ceiling,
And corner cupboards just revealing
Blue plates and platters standing up
And the pale half-moon of a cup.

I think of ships, ghost-white with foam,
Headed down long seas for home,
Their oaken beams and creaking sides
Straining against the wind and tides,
Clean-breasted as a bird in flight
Cleaving the frosty air of night.

I think of Druid priests of old,
Of all the ancient stories told,
Of knights in armor, ladies fair,
Of little cottages, clean air,
Where oak trees spread their branches wide
And grow in majesty and pride.

Edna Jaques

Summer Interlude

A heady odor from sweet clover grass
Blends with the scent of other growing things,
Including flowers summering en masse
Where meadowlarks direct communal sings.

The days are long. Vacationers, relaxed,
Ease out the glory-laden interlude,
Succumb to dreams; no energy is taxed,
For now the land is in a glowing mood.

Its changeful beauty never palls the heart,
For keyed to sun-clad loveliness and peace,
It stretches on, each field a work of art,
To where God's blessings seemingly decrease.

Its toll-free byways ramble here and there
Through upward-reaching tendrils, green and fair.

Lydia O. Jackson

A Father Is So Much More

Elaine C. Frantz

A baby girl is born. Instantaneously, from amid the ranks of ordinary men, there emerges a courageous, fearless, and gallant man who is quaking in his shoes. He holds the newborn to his heart. In the years to come, the child will call him Father. As time goes by, she will come to know that this man is the most extraordinary individual with whom she will ever have the pleasure of being acquainted.

He is no ordinary man who can speak with the knowledge and wisdom of a sage, preparing her for adventures into foreign worlds; who can hear the sound of the sun pushing the clouds out of her world and help her to hear it too; who can touch the stars and pull them a little closer to her; and who can taste the worst cookies that she will make and then eat three or four more from the batch. No, he is no ordinary man, this man she calls her father.

He is no ordinary man who always lives in a state of becoming; who is continually learning from his children; who is made richer by the sight of his children coming home; who teaches that all the pros and cons must be weighed before a decision is made; who stands willingly ready to experience all that he has never done before; who is able to inspire monumental achievements in her; who faces no problems in his life, only difficult situations which are the portals of discovery; who is constantly called upon to be the very strongest one; and who provides the ever-present base to touch when her world is full of confusion and question.

He is no ordinary man who, during the course of his lifetime, has worn many different faces and has been defined in many different ways. Whether viewed by his daughter with the perspective of a child, a teenager, or an adult, he is the focus of a special sort of love.

The father that she knows from her childhood was an all-around man. She thought he did everything better than anyone else. He was going to work, coming home, and building a house. He was caring for his child so much that he would take her everywhere he could, sharing his joys and talents for living.

He was a body shielding her from strangers, big dogs, and noisy things; a broad expanse of chest to nestle against; and a foot to sit on and a leg to hold tightly for a ride around the house. But more than this, he was two strong arms holding her up to touch the sky, to see inside a bird's nest, or to fly like an airplane. Fearlessly, they adventured into realms that held surprise after surprise for her. When he was with her, she was never afraid.

He was there for her debut on the school stage; she could see his smile, surrounded by the rest of the audience. He was there for her first bike ride; his loud applause steadied her.

He brought flowers to tickle her nose, a good-night kiss in the dark when he came home late and thought she was asleep, and an old hat that made her smarter when he put it on her head. He was the builder of wonderful toys, a backyard swing set from old pieces of pipe, backyard ice rinks each winter, model trains for under the Christmas tree, remote-controlled airplanes and boats to play with at the park.

He was proud of pigtails, ponytails, and fancy dresses for dress-up times, but he made certain that he taught his blue-jeaned girl to throw and bat a baseball and to hold her own in races to the finish line.

The father that she knows from her childhood was all this and so much more.

The father that she knows from her teenage years was the giver of wings and the holder of reins. She always loved him although some of her actions may not have assured him of that. He was affectionately called Fossil, as a result of his own suggestion.

He taught her to respect herself and others and to learn from each good or bad experience. He was a man of strong belief, a wealth of truth in the midst of storms of confusion, and a discerning disciplinarian.

He was actively involved in her maturing as an impatient driving instructor, as just another chaperone, and as a coach who could be heard shouting above the din of the crowd at a basketball game. He was the firm cornerstone of the family who gave her values to believe in, a heritage which she felt worthy and willing to maintain, and an urgency for living her life completely.

The father that she knows from her youth was all this and so much more.

The father that she knows in her adulthood is a sensible sage with a streak of craziness who still

lives his life knowing that perfection is elusive, but available. He could slow down a bit, but he won't since he is headed for retirement with a lot of living still to do. Somehow his mere presence continues to trigger the potential in her. He would admit to being pleased with the fruits of his lifetime labors. Yes, he is pleased but not satisfied. An individual cannot be satisfied and evolving at the same time.

The father that she knows in her adulthood is all this and so much more.

To this man she'll be quick to say a hearty, "Happy Father's Day, Dad!" She will kiss him on the cheek, promise herself to share many more moments with him, and present him with a single yellow rose to express the feelings which words cannot. And she'll look foward to growing older with her father, this extraordinary man!

God's Expressions

Look without!
Behold the beauty of the day,
The shout
Of color to glad color,
Rocks and trees
And sun and seas
And wind and sky:
All these
Are God's expression,
Artwork of His hand
Which men must love
Ere they can understand.

Richard Hovey

Loved Things

I love the flowers that fill the gladsome day
And birds that trust in God's providing way;
I listen to the prayer-enchanted brook
That flows to many seas through shaded nook;
I trace the vagrant clouds that pass like life,
Some clear and others filled with hidden strife.
I love cool rains accented by its tears
For growing plants and freshening up the years;
I love soft breeze and sunsets' softened glow
That spread enchanted beauty here below.
I see the soft mist of the evening dew,
Each drop a pearl, sun-kissed to rainbow hue;
I love the home that lives by God's own plan
Of working, sharing to build the race of man.
These loves combined are like the heavenly host
And stand for things of life that I love most.

Mamie Ozburn Odum

Thou Art My Sister; I Love You

Thou art my sister because we were born of the same
Great Spirit, conceived from the same mound of earth.
We slept quietly together in the cradle of unknowing until
He in his gentleness set us in the midst of humanity.
You are my sister; I love you.

You and I are destined to be companions on the highway
of life. Together or apart, you are my sister; I love
you. If the color of my skin is different from yours,
it mattereth not; only let the beauty of our souls be
kindred.

I will honor your wisdom and understanding, as you will
mine. Together we shall seek the seeds of truth in the
distant rooms of the Great Spirit; the reflection of
inner knowledge shall wear as beauty upon our faces.
You are my sister; I love you.

I will be human and fall down in rough places, but thy
hand is near mine. I will reach for it; I shall not be
alone. I will embrace you when the rains of sorrow
visit you. I will befriend your soul as if it were
my own. You are my sister; I love you.

If death takes from me the lamp of life and the veil
of eternal sleep falls across my eyes before yours,
I will wait for you. I will come to lead you across
the bridge of night into the meadows of the Great Spirit.
You are my sister; I love you.

Jean Humphrey Chaillie

Roses

The queen of the flowers blooms in June,
Its fragrance drifting upon the air,
Dew-pearled beneath the summer moon
In lovely colors beyond compare.

Extolled by poets, beloved by brides,
Sweetest of all the summer flowers,
Its fragrance in potpourri abides
To last through winter's long, cold hours.

Behold the rose a message brings,
Pure and sweet, all flowers above,
As through the summer dusk it flings
The heart's sweet memories of Junetime love.

Ruth B. Field

Clematis

Georgia B. Adams

Oh, come see our clematis as
It winds and twines along
Our arbor in the garden
To the tune of summer's song.

A purple mass of flowers,
It shares its wealth with me;
It is June's contribution;
Oh, you must come and see.

I'd love to share its beauty,
And with a wistful sigh,
I wish you'd stop to see it
When you are passing by!

THE RIGHT WAY

Love and Determination

It was the day before the summer vacation, and the Gold house was bristling with excitement. The family was busy packing their suitcases and making last minute preparations for their annual trip to the mountains. The children were scampering around gathering their sporting equipment and getting ready for a fun-filled week of swimming, fishing, ball playing, and hiking in the woods.

Suddenly, twelve-year-old David appeared in his father's bedroom and asked for an old shoe box. He stated that he was looking through the bushes in the yard for a baseball that he had lost the day before, when he suddenly discovered a beautiful yellow finch with a broken wing. He remembered that a bird house in the yard was inhabited by finches. Mr. Gold, well aware of his son's love for animals, anticipated a problem as he handed him the shoe box, and he began to worry that this could be a distraction from his son's vacation plans.

A few moments later David came into the house with a magnificent bird in the shoe box. The bird was in obvious need of some expert attention.

"Who do you think I should call for help?" David asked.

"Well," said Mr. Gold, "I would start with the Society for the Prevention of Cruelty to Animals; they're usually pretty good with things like this."

Within a few moments David was on the telephone explaining his problem to a representative of the local SPCA. After a short conversation, he dejectedly told his father that they could offer little help.

Now David was more determined than ever as he looked at the helpless little creature fluttering in the shoe box. In the hours that followed, he spoke to the local veterinarian, the police department, the pet shop in the center of town, the county agricultural agent, and a farmer that he had once met while working on a school project. But each call had the same conclusion. Everyone was very sympathetic but either too busy or not capable of helping. Their concern was genuine but did not help David's frustration. One man who answered the phone, however, suggested that David try the veterinary school in the nearby city.

With renewed optimism, David quickly dialed the operator to get the number of the college and was soon speaking to a very understanding gentleman and explaining his problem. The man listened with great patience, and then told David that there were many injured animals and birds in the woods and it was impossible to help them all. He advised David to take the little bird back to where he found it and let nature take its course. As David whispered "thank you" and was about to say good-bye, the kindly gentleman asked, "By the way, where do you live, young man?" After a pause, the man said, "I'm going to send you a book on bird care; I think you'll find it interesting."

Very frustrated and dejected and a bit angry, David went up to his room and looked at the little bird that he now felt was doomed.

While he was sitting on his bed, his father came into the room and sat down beside him. "David," he said, "We live in a very difficult world. Although everyone you spoke to would have liked to help, most people don't have the time to answer every call or to help every little bird. I doubt very much if there is anyone who could really help you, but who knows, maybe the wing will heal itself. I bet by the time we get home from our vacation that little fellow will have flown away!"

David forced a little smile and thanked his father for coming in and talking to him. He knew he was right, and he would have to do what the man on the telephone said.

The next day was a beautiful, bright Saturday, and the Gold family had finished packing their car and was waiting for David to come downstairs with the little bird.

Suddenly the front door chimes rang, and Mr. Gold opened the door. There he was greeted by a pleasant looking, middle-aged man who had a small cage in his hand.

"Does David Gold live here?" the man asked.

"Why yes, yes," stammered a surprised Mr. Gold. "Please come in." The entire family was standing at the door with surprised looks on their faces. Just then David came to the door with the shoe box in his hand.

"Hello, David. I'm glad to meet you," said the man. "Thank you for calling. My name is Dr. Robertson, and I am a professor at the University Veterinary School. We're pretty good at fixing broken wings, and I am sure that we'll be able to help your little friend!" With a smile from ear to ear, David handed the doctor the box and shook his hand for several seconds.

As the gentleman turned to leave, Mr. Gold stopped him and said, "Dr. Robertson, can I ask you a question? I must admit that I'm very surprised to see you. How can such a busy person as you take time to help a little bird?"

The professor smiled and looked at David and then said, "Mr. Gold, I didn't come because of the little bird; I came because of the little boy. Any young fellow who would go to all the trouble that your son did just to help a little bird certainly deserves help from somebody. Since I really don't live too far away, I thought I'd drive over and offer my assistance. Who knows, someday David might decide to be a veterinarian and wind up in one of my classes!"

As the Gold family locked up their house and got into the car to start out on their trip, they knew that this was going to be a very special vacation. David had shown them the value of love and determination, an experience that they would never forget.

Dr. Donald R. Stoltz,
President
Norman Rockwell Museum
Philadelphia, PA

Golden Wedding Day

To My Parents

Until we've grown, we never know
   or fully realize
How sweet and kind our parents are,
How gentle and how wise.

We simply take for granted,
From day to passing day,
Each sacrifice they make for us
In their own loving way.

But then we grow and finally learn,
The way that children do,
How much their love
   has really meant,
How thoughtful they've been, too.

And so this comes with all the thanks
You both deserve, and more,
For there aren't two dearer parents
Than the ones this day is for.

Parents are those special people
Who teach us how to love.
They begin their role
   with heads full of plans,
Hearts full of dreams,
   and arms full with
   a squirming little bundle of life.

Busy from sunup to sundown,
Their sleep is interrupted
   by the hungry cries
Of a tiny person with a
   very large appetite.

Through the years, parents become
   teachers, counselors, and comforters
   and seem to keep going on
   an endless supply of courage,
   humor, and love—mostly love.

It shows in everything they do,
From grocery shopping
   to family outings.

It's what overcomes those moments
   of spilled milk and muddy shoes
   and broken windows.

Parents never get repaid for all they do,
   but they seem to be fulfilled.
And though their rewards consist mostly of
   hugs and kisses and "We love yous,"
   they are more thankful for these
   than anything else.

And as time passes
   and childhood gives way
   to understanding,
We know beyond a doubt
   that parents themselves
   are far more precious than gold.

On your Golden Wedding Day,
Thank you for being the
   wonderful parents you are.

Bonnie Rusk

And what is so rare as a day in June?
Then, if ever, come perfect days;
Then heaven tries the earth if it be in tune,
And over it softly her warm ear lays;
Whether we look, or whether we listen,
We hear life murmur or see it glisten;
Every clod feels a stir of might,
An instinct within it that reaches and towers,
And, groping blindly above it for light,
Climbs to a soul in grasses and flowers.

June

The flush of life may well be seen
Thrilling back over hills and valleys;
The cowslip startles in meadows green,
The buttercup catches the sun in its chalice,
And there's never a leaf nor a blade too mean
To be some happy creature's palace.

The little bird sits at his door in the sun,
Atilt like a blossom among the leaves,
And lets his illumined being o'errun
With the deluge of summer it receives.
His mate feels the eggs beneath her wings,
And the heart in her dumb breast flutters and sings;
He sings to the wide world, and she to her nest—
In the nice ear of nature, which song is the best?

James Russell Lowell

Yellow Is the Color of Summer

Yellow is the color of summer;
Surely it is so
When black-eyed Susans and buttercups
As mini-suns brightly glow.

I see it in the hearts of daisies,
The skin of a ripening pear,
Corn on the cob at picnics,
Wisps of baby hair.

Yellow is happy and shining,
A carousel ride all the while.
Yellow, the color of summer,
I see
In your sunny smile.

Violet Bigelow Rourke

Always Close

Michele Arrieh

A stranger came to live at my house when I was a year old. She had curly hair and a round face with large dark eyes. When I got to know her better, we became the greatest of friends. My new little sister, as my mother told me, was the best present I could ever receive—a true companion and ally for life. At the time I couldn't understand the meaning of her words, but the ensuing years of sharing and growing together resulted in one of the dearest and closest friendships I'll ever know.

To begin with, she was impossible to avoid. We shared the same room at home for years, sleeping at first in twin cribs and then in twin beds. Our domain saw some struggles as well as peaceful cohabitation. At one time the conflict grew so intense that we drew an imaginary line down the carpet in the middle of our room and had to ask each other's permission to step over it.

Of course, since I was the older, more sensible one, I was understanding when my sister requested that she share my bed on nights when she felt the boogeyman or another equally horrible monster was lurking in the closet. I always insisted there was no such thing even though she could never persuade me to open the closet door to prove my point.

At the innocent age of four, I experienced my first encounter with guilt and remorse over an accidental injury I inflicted on my sister. I was playing "drop the tin can" off the third-story porch of the building where we lived. When my sister happened to walk by underneath, I shouted "catch" and threw a half-opened can down just as she stopped and gazed upward, completely transfixed. The razor-sharp lid cut quite a gash on the side of her nose, and she was rushed to the hospital before I realized what had happened. Even now my sister bears a hairline scar there, but she never, even jokingly, reminds me of the incident nor carries the slightest grudge.

Of course, there were times when she caused just as much trouble for me. One summer afternoon she was the leader in what could have been an unintentional suicide pact. Our favorite medicine when we were children was orange-flavored children's aspirin. One day when my mother was cleaning the medicine cabinet, my sister snatched the bottle of aspirin and brought it outdoors where I was playing with a friend. At first the three of us didn't know how to open the "child-proof" cap, but, always innovative, my sister smashed the bottle on the concrete pavement, releasing dozens of the tiny orange tablets. We then proceeded to swallow every last one in a race to see who could eat the most! We also thought we could cleverly conceal the evidence of the theft. My mother had already discovered the missing aspirin, however, and was instinctively approaching in our direction. That evening, as we each took our spoonfuls of ipecac, we discovered what an unpleasant experience "releasing" the evidence could be.

For most of our childhood, since we were so close in age, our mother dressed us alike. As we grew older, it became increasingly embarrassing to be dressed like twins; so gradually we refused to accept duplicate clothes. This also gave us the added advantage of having a double wardrobe since we eventually grew to be the same size and could wear each other's clothing. Our parents were fortunate that we didn't quarrel, as many sisters do, over borrowing apparel.

For some reason, there wasn't the usual disruptive sibling rivalry between us either. A little sideward glance from time to time was enough to keep us on our toes. For the most part, we each took pride in the other's achievements. If I excelled in ballet lessons, she did better than I in piano lessons; if I found it easier to paint pictures, she had less trouble learning how to sew.

A type of competitiveness was my sister's "me too" attitude which she displayed in her younger years. This consisted of wanting to do what I was doing at the same time which proved to be difficult since our age difference always kept me one step ahead of her. When I went to grade school, high school, and college before she did, she felt left behind and very dissatisfied. Of course, she eventually caught up and, in the process, did quite well. Somehow, my forging the new territory always made the path easier for her to tread.

Recently, my sister entered an entirely new phase that has changed our relationship but not lessened the closeness we feel toward each other. One day—without much warning it seemed—she married and moved five hundred miles away! As I stood at her side at the altar on her wedding day, a hundred images flashed through my mind, mostly all the memories we will recall throughout our lives. I knew I'd always cherish my childhood playmate, my partner in crime, my close confidante, my best friend. The day went so fast that I hardly had time to tell her what I was feeling, but anyone could tell by my glistening eyes that the thought was there.

In Flame and Fire

Alice Leedy Mason

Friendship is like the mist that drapes the hills.
It covers jarring heights, the rocks, the spills,
Showing only sky, a blue arc etched above,
To which the high hills shout their song of love.
Courage comes to climb when well-worn paths are gone
And one true friend can urge the traveler on.

There is a quietness friendship recalls:
Old books from dusty shelves, long silent halls,
Two voices whispering, a closing gate,
Soft bells that lift the heartstrings soon and late.
Two friends recall an old familiar place,
A special time, a sweet remembered face.

There is an understanding known to friends
That on no fact or point of law depends.
A gentle touch, a smile along the way
Can walk the heart above the press of day.
Given time, the world is sure to see
A splendid strength, a quiet dignity.

"Gather each sunny hour" those fragile things
That bear the mark of shared rememberings:
A stolen glance, some sound advice outspoken,
A rose to give, applause, a token—
A meteor in blazing flight descends
To write in flame and fire, GODSPEED TO FRIENDS!

ACKNOWLEDGMENTS

THOU ART MY SISTER; I LOVE YOU by Jean Humphrey Chaillie. (Previously published twice.) Originally published as "You Are My Sister" in THE PHOENIX REDSKIN, Phoenix Indian High School, Copyright © 1964 by the United States Department of the Interior, Bureau of Indian Affairs. Reprinted by permission in ARIZONA HIGHWAYS MAGAZINE, Copyright © 1978 by The Arizona Department of Transportation. SUMMER INTERLUDE by Lydia O. Jackson. Published originally in the July 1966 issue of THE AMERICAN POET. FOR LITTLE GIRLS by Jane Merchant. From her book HALFWAY UP THE SKY. Published by Abingdon Press. Used through courtesy of Elizabeth Merchant. Our sincere thanks to the following author whose address we were unable to locate: Belle S. Mooney for PLEA OF THE CHILDREN.

COLOR ART AND PHOTO CREDITS
(in order of appearance)

Front and back cover, Garden near Brocham Green, Surrey, England, Colour Library International (USA) Limited; inside front cover, Washington daisies, Olympic Peninsula, Washington, Ed Cooper; Petunias, William A. Holmes; Smiles in the sun, Freelance Photographers Guild; Strawberries, Fred Sieb; Friendship garden, Hampfler Studios; Floral garden scene, western Pennsylvania, William A. Holmes; Shared laughter, Colour Library International (USA) Limited; New arrivals, H. Armstrong Roberts; Getting along, H. Armstrong Roberts; Colorful bouquet, Bob Taylor; The daisy's decision, Robert Cushman Hayes; Time for tea, Fred Sieb; At Grandmother's house, Three Lions, Inc.; "Friend Ship," Camden Harbor, Maine, Fred Sieb; Quiet reflection, Freelance Photographers Guild; Forest floor, Fern Canyon, Redwood National Park, J. Carrillo; Rustic setting, Bob Taylor; Rose garden, John Neubauer; Clematis, Fred Sieb; THE RIGHT WAY, Norman Rockwell; Scenic Marlow, New Hampshire, Freelance Photographers Guild; Mill stream in Leverett, Massachusetts, Freelance Photographers Guild; Roadside beauty, H. Armstrong Roberts; Sunset in Phoenix, Arizona, Tom Stack; inside back cover, H. Armstrong Roberts.

A Special Issue . . .

The upcoming issue of IDEALS is the Countryside issue. It's a special issue because it allows you the opportunity to explore our great land from sea to shining sea and from mountain-top to desert floor and, of course, the heartland of our countryside that we hold so dear.

We feature the best-loved poet, William Wordsworth, along with poetry that represents the charm of the country's rolling hills, the desert plains, the seaside and the small hometowns that bring to mind pleasant memories.

Your letters tell us that you look forward to your upcoming issues of IDEALS. But we might ask, isn't there a loved one, a shut-in or cherished friend who might appreciate them just as much as you do? IDEALS serves to provide a wonderful gift that reminds our friends that we are thinking of them on at least eight special occasions throughout the year.

Please remember, IDEALS is a wonderful way to share the beautiful world we live in with family and friends.